ENCHANTED LAND
NEW MEXICO

Photography by Harvey Caplin

Descriptions by Ruth Armstrong

Bank Securities, Inc.
in collaboration with
Calvin Horn Publisher, Inc.
Albuquerque, New Mexico

Calvin Horn Publisher, Inc.
Albuquerque, New Mexico

ISBN 910750-28-9
Library of Congress Card No. 73-83962

Manufactured in the United States of America

For Grace — whose patience, under-
standing and many lonely hours made
it all possible.

CONTENTS

FOREWORD

New Mexico is a growing, progressive state — a blending of people and cultures of many races and national backgrounds. The impact of this is change — fast-growing cities, skylines that change by the year or even month; super-highways that crisscross the once-meandering trails of Indian and trader.

The personality of New Mexico is changing. Yet the essential character of our state is as unchanging as the great spires of the Organ Mountains or the familiar face of Old Baldy.

The deep blue of turquoise skies is still ours to savor. The sparkling gold of Autumn still tints the aspens. The marvels of sun, silence and adobe are still a way of life in New Mexico — even amidst the hustle and bustle of a fast-moving economy.

The essential New Mexico is still ours to enjoy: the mountain trails, the fishing streams, the magnificence of mountain scenery, the sparkling air of early morning, the aura of history that pervades our land. Even the civilizations of the past blend into our landscape and our heritage and spark our imaginations.

The people who came before us left a precious heritage and a fine example of harmonious living and strong relationship with Mother Nature. This is a key to New Mexico's character.

Bank Securities, Inc., representing more than 600 employees and many stockholders, operates in more than 50 locations throughout New Mexico, and thus has strong ties and pleasant rapport with New Mexico's traditions and its past as it serves its future.

It is with pleasure that BSI sponsors, in collaboration with Calvin Horn Publisher, Inc., this fine volume of photographs that depicts the resplendent beauty and character of our Land of Enchantment. Harvey Caplin with his photographs and Ruth Armstrong with her text have captured the essence of New Mexico and the heritage we all want to preserve.

Ted A. Bonnell, President
Bank Securities, Inc.

INTRODUCTION

New Mexico is big and sometimes brutal. It is not for the timid. But once you have come to know it, no other place will satisfy you.

Even though a European civilization was established here twenty-one years before the Pilgrims landed at Plymouth Rock, each newcomer to the state today feels that he, personally, discovered it.

New Mexico is a land of contrasts . . . high plateaus, alpine meadows, semi-desert, gentle valleys, snow-capped peaks and brilliant, jagged cliffs. The people, too, offer contrast. An ancient Indian ceremonial or a Spanish fiesta takes place in the shadow of an atomic installation where brilliant research scientists are probing the future.

The average elevation of the state is 5,700 feet which gives a cool freshness to the air even though the sun may be hot. The clear atmosphere, whipped cream clouds, incredibly blue sky, rugged mountains, earth colors and sunsets of a brilliance to make the eye ache. These are food for the artist and writer.

In color New Mexico challenges the eye. In black and white it dares the mind to grasp it.

— Ruth Armstrong

PART I
SCENIC NEW MEXICO

From the snow-capped peaks of northern New Mexico to the cactus-studded plateaus of the south stretches a boundless source of beauty and inspiration. High elevation, constant sunshine, air so clear it snaps — all combine to make an ideal climate.

Though one of the youngest states, New Mexico is the seat of the oldest European civilization in this country. Almost a quarter of a century before the Pilgrims landed, Spanish colonists were tilling the soil of New Mexico. A hundred and fifty years before the famous missions of California and Texas were built, massive adobe missions were built in New Mexico.

New Mexico is today a graceful blending of several cultures, with much of the best of each. The color and contrast of this vast country never lose their appeal to those lucky enough to live here.

Shimmering aspen trees reflected in a beaver pond spread living gold over
the mountain sides of New Mexico in October.

The stillness of a mountain pool is broken only by the leap of a rainbow trout
6   or the slap of a beaver's tail.

You have but to climb a tree to touch a cloud. Almost every summer afternoon big white thunderheads build up and scatter refreshing showers over mountains, valleys and mesas.

7

8   Feathery heads of pampas grass give shape and motion to the wind.

Who needs asphalt?

10   The nine Latir Lakes are like a giant string of emeralds flung into the mountains
of Carson National Forest.

Where you can see a hundred miles and think to eternity . . . finite man is nearest his Maker on top of a mountain.

The yucca is the State Flower of New Mexico. It's Spanish name, Vela de Dios, "Candle of the Lord," seems best suited to its stately elegance. The Indians found it most utilitarian. From its roots they made soap; its succulent seed pods they used for food, and from its tough spears or leaves they extracted fibers used in making rope and weaving baskets.

12

Shiprock — legendary rock of the Navajos. Many years ago before time began a giant bird gathered The People (as the Navajos call themselves) on its back and carried them to a chosen high land of red rocks and long views. The bird is Shiprock, silent and weird in the changing light.

13

Cleopatra's Needle, a spire of red sandstone, pierces the sky of the rugged mesa country that is part of the Navajo reservation in the northwestern part of the State.

Soda Dam across the Jemez River has been built up through countless ages
by minerals in the mountain stream. 15

An arroyo (Spanish word for gully) is a dry, sandy, innocent looking stream bed — most of the time. When a sudden afternoon shower falls it can immediately produce a "flash flood," a wall of water four or five feet high that can wash cars, people, horses or boulders along like pebbles.

Valle Grande, where cattle graze contentedly on lush green grass and drink
from icy streams of melted snow, was once the raging furnace of a volcano. 17

18   Mountains in the southern part of the State are rugged and stark, reflecting colors of the sky and sunset. These were the strongholds of Apache warriors.

Relics of another day speak of the pioneers who crossed New Mexico to reach the gold of California.

The White Sands are not sand, but gypsum — dazzling, undulating, ever-changing dunes of pure white. Animal life on the dunes has adapted to its environment by becoming white.

20

Atop Enchanted Mesa on the Acoma reservation a group of Indians was
marooned and held there by the attacking warriors until they starved to death
— so the legend goes. The red earth of the mesa country cracks under the
drying sun in a pattern of sculptured carpeting.

22   The fishing is good . . . the meditation is better high in the Jemez Mountains.

The legendary Rio Grande cuts through a volcanic mesa before it widens out in the fertile valleys below.

24   Right at timberline, this lake high in the Sangre de Cristo Mountains can be reached only on foot or horseback.

Winter snows and summer showers replenish the mountain streams with clear, icy water.

How many ages has it taken the Rio Grande to gouge its way through this harsh volcanic plateau?

PART II
RECREATION THAT RE-CREATES

The entire state of New Mexico is a vast recreation area filled with monuments to history. Only a few of its hundreds of points of scenic or historic interest are formally marked or set aside. There are eight state monuments, ten national monuments, one national park and thirty-two state parks. They range all the way from Folsom site where remains of prehistoric man 10,000 years old were found, to lakes where water skiing and fishing lure the sportsmen.

Year-round sunshine encourages people to explore and have fun. Amateur archaeologists like to prowl around old ruins. High mountains offer some of the best skiing, hiking and camping in the country. Trout in mountain streams entice the fishermen. Because New Mexico is one of the least known and understood states, newcomers and visitors are infected with the enthusiasm of discovery.

Climbing a mountain is not always just a form of recreation. It is sometimes a sphere of operation for a rescue team such as this led by a Presbyterian minister who interprets his commission to save lost souls in the most literal sense.

Loose shingles and torn screen doors echo in the breezes that blow through
Madrid, once an important coal mining town.

A rich silver strike created Shakespeare, but what poet named it? The name "Stratford" . . . "Avon" . . . are still visible on peeling signs in this adobe ghost town, strangely incongruous with its name.

There is no quiet as deep as that of a sunny morning after a fierce storm. 31

In wintertime a deep mantle of snow settles over the mountains, delighting skiers as well as farmers who depend on it to irrigate their fields the next

summer.

Sandia Peak tram rises 2.7 miles up the rugged western face of the Sandia Mountains near Albuquerque. In 15 minutes skiers can be at the crest, ready to ski down the other side.

33

Pack trips into the wilderness areas of New Mexico are a matchless form of recreation in the truest sense . . . re-creation.

The Cumbres and Toltec Scenic Railroad, a narrow gauge relic of bygone days, takes passengers over mountains, valleys and spectacular gorges on its way from Chama, New Mexico, to Antonito, Colorado.

36   There are high mountain lakes in all parts of New Mexico where the fishing
is great. Streams and lakes at lower elevations are a little more accessible.

The Land of Contrasts is nowhere more vividly portrayed than by this snowfall
on the badlands of a fossil bed.

37

Twelve ski areas in New Mexico, from Raton in the north to Cloudcroft in the south, offer excellent skiing.

Clear dry air makes for good powder snow. The season generally lasts from Thanksgiving to April, but it can vary as much as a month, either direction.   39

Many mountainous areas of New Mexico are perfect for snowmobiling . . . on the gentler mountain slopes away from the steeper ski slopes. Chama, in the northern part of the state, is the snowmobile center of New Mexico.

Cross country skiing, as well as downhill skiing, is a major winter sport in most of the state. 41

42 Trout fishing for rainbow or the native cutthroat is great in the streams and lakes of the mountains of New Mexico.

With man's intense desire today for privacy and natural beauty, back packing
has opened up a whole new world for those who prefer solitude to regimentation.   43

Millions of acres of National Forest land in New Mexico are ideal for snowmobiling or snowshoe hiking.

44

Included in the National Forests of New Mexico are four wilderness areas —
Pecos, Gila, San Pedro and Wheeler Peak Wilderness Areas — where the pristine
beauty of the mountains is preserved for man to enjoy for generations to come.   45

Some noise is all right . . . like the tumbling roar of a mountain stream, or a scream of delight when you hook a big one.

Many youngsters in New Mexico learn to ride almost as soon as they learn to walk. Some develop great skill in horse shows and other competitive events.

48 Whether a 'dude' or a native westerner, a chuck wagon supper at sunset at the foot of a desert mountain is an experience to remember.

Horseracing is one of the most popular spectator sports in the state. Seasons at the State's five major tracks are staggered to make it available most of the year.

49

50   Horseback riding is just plain, sociable western fun.

Navajo Lake in northwestern New Mexico backs up 15,000 acres of sparkling blue water behind Navajo Dam. Eleven other major lakes in the state offer boating facilities.

Pack trips into the high country above timerline take man away from the problems of every-day living. Wheeler Peak north of Taos is 13,161 feet high, and the highest point in the state.

At Chaco Canyon are hundreds of archaeological sites unequalled in North America, the largest of which is D-shaped Pueblo Bonito which had over 800 rooms and is the most impressive example of masonry in the southwest. Indians lived here from the seventh through the twelfth centuries.

Carlsbad Caverns National Park, near Carlsbad in southeastern New Mexico is an underground fairyland of limestone formations, still a-making. Thousands upon thousands of years older than the memory of mankind, these fantastic creations speak of universal patience.

PART III
THE WORLD OF THE COWBOY

The world of the cowboy is a real one. It is no figment of a fiction writer's imagination. It is a purposeful, down-to-earth way of making a living that they happen to like.

The "wild and wooly" west so often romanticized in stories is based on approximately the last twenty-five years of the past century. No other quarter century in recorded history has so captured the romantic fancy of a nation as that period when frontier towns were being established in the west and law and order had not quite caught up with the people. It is true that there were range wars, gun fights, hangings and wild saloon fights. But it is also true that there were ranchers and cowboys who never wore a gun or went to a necktie party.

Today's cattlemen are business men. Some live in cities and have an office. Some inspect their holdings from an airplane or a Jeep, but the backbone of the cattle industry is still, as it always has been, the cowboy on his horse.

If generalizations are valid, you might say that cowboys as a rule are unassuming, hard-working, honest and humorous. The beauty and serenity of their surroundings must have some influence on their characters.

Today's cowboy is not the swaggering gun slinger of fiction. He is the quiet outdoorsman who is invigorated by physical exercise and the wide expanses of his horizons.

Roads don't always lead to where the wagons must go. Steep mountainsides, rocky hills, cactus-studded plateaus must give the cowboys a feeling of kinship with pioneers of a hundred years ago whose uncharted paths crossed the same terrain.

A cowboy's clothes are for a reason: boots whose pointed toes find the stirrup and whose heels hold them there; leather chaps and heavy, long-sleeved shirts to protect against underbrush; tight pants that keep his skin from being rubbed off; wide-brimmed hats to shade his eyes and face from the glare of a brilliant sun.

Breaking a bronc is part of the normal activity of a working cowboy. On larger cattle ranches there will sometimes be as many as 200 horses in the working string.

New Mexico is a state of large cattle ranches — some covering as much as 400,000 acres. Many have grazing permits on adjoining forest lands.

A "cutting horse," usually a Quarterhorse, is trained to cut a particular animal out of a herd. He must be especially intelligent and responsive.

Home is where the wagon is. The chuck wagon is under a tent and when on the move, carries the bed rolls as well as the food. The "hoodlum" wagon carries tents, stakes, barrels of water and other supplies. The cowboys sleep in tents or under the stars if they prefer.

Around the chuckwagon the cook's word is the last one. Beef is the most important item of diet, and there's plenty of it. Meals, usually two a day, are cooked in Dutch ovens. Eggs are hauled in barrels of grain for safekeeping.

64   Lonely, stark, miles away from home or highway, sentinels of the range faithfully pump water into the tanks. Even a moderate breeze can set the blades a-turning.

Prime rib roasts and T-bone steaks on the hoof.

"Round-up time" are not just words of a song. Round-up is the harvest of
a valuable crop. Through summer's heat and winter's snow the cattle are carefully
tended and prepared for shipment to market.

A rope in the hands of a seasoned cowboy is sheer magic. At branding time he eases in quietly and cuts the calf away from the herd, then throws his lasso so the top of the loop hits the calf's flank. When the calf jumps, the loop goes under the hind legs and he is brought down and unceremoniously dragged to the branding iron.

70 How would *you* like to geld this half ton of kicking fury?

Some of the big ranchers own thousands of sheep, but there are many small ranchers who own small flocks. Indian pueblos (villages) have communal herds, and most of the Spanish -American farmers have small flocks. The three items brought in by the Spanish conquistadors that changed life in the Southwest more than anything else were probably sheep, horses and metal.

72   Wall to wall Wilton — on the hoof.

Rivalry between sheep and cattle ranchers has provided the basis for many a range war. Because sheep crop off the grass so much shorter than cattle do, they can ruin range land if not controlled properly. Nowdays many large cattle ranches also raise sheep, and by rotating the herds and ranges, can practice duel use of the range, that is, graze cattle and sheep both.

PART IV
THE FIRST NEW MEXICANS

For at least 25,000 years man has lived in New Mexico. Traces of Folsom, Clovis and Sandia Man have all been found here. When the Spaniards first came in 1540 they found the Indians divided into two general classifications: the Pueblo Indians who were sedentary farmers living in communities mostly along the Rio Grande valley; and the war-like nomadic tribes such as the Navajos and Apaches who hunted and raided the peaceful pueblos.

The Indians adjusted to Spanish, and later American, rule, but have succeeded in maintaining a strong identity. They perform ancient ceremonial rituals which are beautiful to behold and meaningful to them. During Spanish days most of the Indians accepted the Christian religion — but as an overlay to and not in place of their ancient beliefs. Their closeness to nature is expressed in their ceremonials where they often masquerade as animals and birds, in their prayers for rain and fertility.

The Indian culture is important and highly respected in New Mexico.

The multi-storied pueblo at Taos is more reminiscent of the ancient dwellings than any other pueblo today. The Taos art colony, founded in the nearby village of Taos, set a standard that has given this region a reputation among the world's artists.

The Navajos are the largest Indian tribe in America. In the past century they have increased from about 10,000 to over 100,000. Their reservation covers over 15 million acres of land in New Mexico, Arizona and Utah.

Corn was one of the staple foods of the Indians long before the Spaniards came. Navajo men are world-famous as silversmiths. This Navajo grandmother and child are wearing hundreds of dollars worth of turquoise and silver jewelry.

Navajo women are as much at home on a pony as their men folk are. Still semi-nomadic, their hogans (hexagon-shaped homes of logs and mud) are scattered over the reservation. Today many of them own pick-up trucks which make the weekly or monthly trip to the trading post.

79

The Spaniards introduced sheep to America, and they have been firmly adopted by the Navajos whose nomadic way of life makes them natural shepherds.

Navajo rugs are famous for beauty and durability. First they shear the sheep, wash, card, spin and dye the wool, and then weave the rug. A 3 by 5 foot rug requires an average of 350 hours of work.

84   These little girls are all dressed up in costumes typical of the Plains Indians.

Navajos gather from vast areas of their reservation for a "sing," or curing cere-
mony. These complicated ceremonies may last from one to nine nights.

The "olla carriers" — always a hit in parades when they depict the old ritual of carrying water pots on their heads.

Much of the Navajo Reservation is high plateau land punctuated by sandstone cliffs and buttes, but there are also several mountain ranges within their reservation.

Apache women, like their cousins the Navajos, use the cradle board to carry their babies. However, unlike the Navajos, they are no longer nomadic. Instead, they live in conventional towns on their beautiful mountainous reservations.

The Devil Dance suggests the once fierce nature of the Apaches. They produced such famous warriors as Cochise, Geronimo and Victorio. There are two Apache reservations in New Mexico — the Mescalero and the Jicarilla, where they live peacefully as ranchers and farmers.

Clothing, hair style and facial characteristics of the Taos Indians resemble the Plains Indians more than any other Pueblo group. Even their beaded moccasins suggest the Plains Indians.

Drum makers of Cochiti Pueblo are considered to be the best makers of ceremonial drums — hollowed-out trunks of cottonwood trees, laced with raw hide. This drummer stands atop the kiva or ceremonial chamber which is entered by the ladder through a hole in the roof.

91

Maria of San Ildefonso Pueblo is the undisputed queen of potters. Her age and eyesight prevent her making pottery now, but her grandson has the same incredible talent for shape and design. Any piece made by Maria is a collector's item.

On ordinary days this young Jemez Indian may be a school teacher, bookkeeper, or truck driver, but on a ceremonial dance day he is an Eagle. Most of the summer dances have to do with crops and rain, and winter dances are mostly hunting dances. Contrary to what many people suppose, dances performed in a pueblo are never done as a tourist attraction.

Most winter dances performed in the pueblos are animal or hunting dances. They are a prayer for good hunting and ample food, and a plea for forgiveness to the animals for having to kill them.

Acoma, the Sky City, one of the most dramatic of all the Indian Pueblos, is built on top of a rock mesa rising 400 feet above the floor of the valley. Most of the Acomans now live in the valley and raise cattle.

95

96   Zuni silversmiths are noted for their skill in the use of turquoise, coral, jet, mother-of-pearl, tortoise shell and steer horn inlaid in silver.

Winter animals dances at the Rio Grande Pueblos usually coincide with the celebration of Christmas, though they pre-date Christianity.

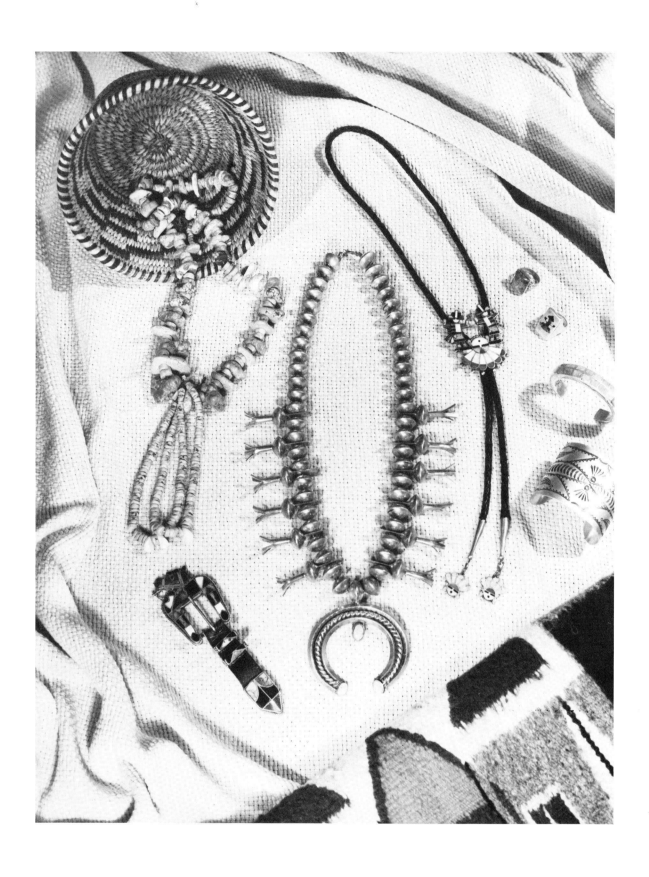

Though in recent years there has been considerable interchange of styles and materials, the Navajos are still best known for their heavy, simple silver jewelry; the Zunis for intricate inlay and the Santo Domingos for bead and shell work.

Most Indian jewelry continues to follow traditional designs, but some craftsmen experiment with new ideas, and change gradually takes place.

The Navajos got sheep from the Spaniards and learned weaving from the Pueblo Indians, and soon became masters at blanket and rug weaving. Rug designs are without significance, but certain patterns have taken on names of the areas where they are produced.

PART V
CHURCHES AND MISSIONS

Civilization, in our terms, begins when man begins to be concerned with something higher than his stomach.

The ancient Indian dwellers in New Mexico developed a deep and abiding religious sense in that they recognized forces and needs larger than themselves. Theirs was an imaginative and happy religion, not dependent upon human sacrifice such as was practiced by ancient tribes in Mexico and Central America. During the Great Pueblo period they developed beautiful forms of art as well as religion, in their pottery, masonry and weaving.

Early Spanish explorers carried the banner of Christian faith along with the flag of Spain. They claimed all they saw (and much they didn't) for "God and King." The first thing they did at each new settlement was to build a church of some sort, even if it were but a bower of branches in which to place a statue of a patron saint.

Faith was what gave the friars courage to remain alone in an isolated and strange world. At a time when great cathedrals were being built in Europe, cathedrals of a different sort were being built in New Mexico. They were made of mud or stone — whatever was at hand. They were massive and stark with little ornamentation. During the Indian Rebellion of 1680 all the mission churches except a half dozen were completely destroyed. But the mark was on the country, and today New Mexico is still a land of churches.

For more than a hundred years the early Spanish missionaries attempted to substitute their religion for the rituals of the Indians. In 1680 the Indians rose in rebellion against both civil and ecclesiastic authority and drove out or killed all the Spaniards. All churches were destroyed or desecrated. When the Spaniards reconquered New Mexico, it was with a wiser heart. Since then the Christian religion has been something of an addition to, rather than in place of, the the ancient beliefs of the Indians.

The mission church at Quarai was built during the 1620's and early 1630's and used only a few years before the entire pueblo was abandoned about 1675 because of incessant raids by the fierce Plains Indians.

Only two of the more than 80 churches built before the rebellion of 1680 remain in use today. One of these is San Estevan, built about 1629, at Acoma. Its massive stone and adobe walls are a monument to the faith of the men who built them. The Acoma Indians still use this magnificent church as their place of worship.

San Estevan Mission at Acoma required a tremendous amount of labor and dedication to construct. Every timber, most of the stones, mud and water had to be carried up 400 feet from the surrounding valley and distant mountains. Enclosed within the walls was once a quiet monastery garden where the Franciscan father cultivated grapes and fruit trees.

An important part of every Indian Pueblo is its church. Usually made of adobe, their gently undulating walls have the appearance of being lovingly molded by hand.

106

The seldom-photographed church at Santo Domingo Pueblo has a distinctively decorated portico and entrance. Like most pueblo churches the adobe wall encloses a burial ground. When the Spaniards first came to New Mexico in 1598 they established Santo Domingo as the ecclesiastic headquarters for the Franciscan missionaries.

107

108 San Miguel Mission in Santa Fe is built over the foundation of an earlier church
that was constructed about 1610, the year the city was founded.

The massive church at Ranchos de Taos is considered by many the most beautiful
Spanish church in the Southwest. Standing magnificently against a background
of mountains rising over 13,000 feet into an intensely blue sky, it dominates
the Taos valley. It was built in 1772, during the same period that Father Junipero
Serra was establishing the California missions.

109

This is all that remains of the original church built at Taos Pueblo in the early 1600's. It was destroyed in the rebellion of 1680 when the Indians either killed or drove out the Spaniards.

El Santuario de Chimayo is one of the favorite shrines of New Mexico. In a small room off the nave a hole in the earthen floor goes down to a spring that has miraculous healing powers. The walls are lined with crutches and braces left there by the faithful.

Spanish and Indian buildings always seem to grow from the earth that surrounds them, whether they are of earth or stone. Santa Maria Mission on the edge of the Acoma Reservation is built of the same stone as the rocky hillside on which it rests.

This is one of many small private chapels in Northern New Mexico. No matter how small, a church is still where a devout man comes to seek forgiveness for his sins, solace for his grief, and courage for tomorrow.

For more than three centuries bells on mission churches in New Mexico have
been calling the faithful to worship.

114

Whether depicted in primitive folk art or in handsome sculpture, Our Lady of Guadalupe, patron saint of New Mexico, is greatly revered.

Religious folk art of 17th and 18th century New Mexico was used to grace the walls of mission churches, home chapels and shrines. Rare old pieces are in museums or private collections, but modern santeros (saint makers) still produce work very much like that their ancestors made.

The church and pueblo at Pecos were abandoned in 1838, but the ruins are preserved as a National Monument.

PART VI
THE CHANGING LANDSCAPE

As New Mexico grows in population, there are many changes in the landscape. Signs of new industry appear: oil derricks, refineries, behemoth machinery, super highways, changing skylines.

All these are subjects for the Caplin camera, too.

Natural resources of New Mexico are great — but not inexhaustible. Oil, gas, mining and timber are among its important industries.

The oil fields in the southeastern part of the State tap the great Permian Basin. 121

122   Drilling for gas in the northwestern part of the State.

Gas fields of New Mexico are a major source of supply for the Southwest and California.

The Chino Mines of Kennecott Copper Company near Silver City are like a
man-made grand canyon. The "Kneeling Nun" on the horizon has been a landmark since the days of the Conquistadors.

124

Deep in the Chino copper mines another level is blasted away to expose the
copper-bearing ore.

125

It takes big equipment to work a big mine. First worked by the Spaniards and Indians two and three centuries ago in small surface mines, this immense operation would have been beyond belief for them.

A copper smelter in southwestern New Mexico processes the ore from the Chino mines.

128   Signs of modern man's conquest of the high mesas now dot the landscape.

PART VII
PEOPLE, PLACES AND THINGS

In every photographer's collection there are shots that he likes for one reason or another: an art subject, friendly people, unusual animal shots, unique landscape.

In the concluding pages are a miscellany of such shots that Photographer Caplin liked — and hopes you will, too.

Jan Clayton, star of movies and television, enjoys the simple life in her home town of Tularosa.

One of New Mexico's most glamorous citizens is Greer Garson. She and her husband, Buddy Fogelson, own the Forked Lightning Ranch near Pecos. They have been instrumental in establishing the Greer Garson Theater at the College of Santa Fe.

132   Spanish dancers in the plaza in Old Albuquerque recall days of grace and romance.

Fort Union National Monument is a memorial to the men who won the West. It protected pioneers from Indian attacks on their westward trek, and was a supply center for many other forts in the Southwest. During the Civil War it played a key role in turning back the Confederate Army that came near to capturing the entire territory.

134 The parade ground at Fort Union echoes only with the memories of soldiers and their wives who lived there in the latter half of the past century.

The plaza in Old Albuquerque has been an important stopping place since 1706. Spanish ox cart caravans laboriously plodding to Mexico, Santa Fe Trail traders, soldiers in Kearney's army, Franciscan padres . . . all have passed this way.

135

136 From the jail on the second floor of old Lincoln County Courthouse, Billy the Kid escaped, killing two officers as he did it.

Patience, friend. It's all in a day's work.

Chile is more than a relish or garnish. It is a way of life that any New Mexican
becomes addicted to very quickly.

Add a bit of moisture to a bit of cold to a bit of pine bough . . . you have
art in its purest form.

El Morro National Monument was a landmark on trails used by Indians, Spanish
conquistadors, wagon trains of pioneers, and soldiers from the forts of the
southwest.

El Morro, or Inscription Rock, has hundreds of signatures carved into its sandstone face. Except for ancient Indian petroglyphs, the oldest inscription was placed there in 1605 by Don Juan de Onate, first governor of New Mexico.

141

One of the lovliest dances performed by the Pueblo Indians is the Butterfly
142 Dance, and why not, with a model such as this.

Man comes and goes and leaves a transient trail. The earth and sky remain.   143